THE UNBREA

CHAPTER 1

Alexis was walking home from work and she realized she forgotten her key at her job she said man now I have to make the trip all the way back. She called her sister Alicia to tell her she was going to be late coming home and she said okay I'll just wait up for you. Then as she hanged up the phone she saw a strange looking man peeping into her job window she walks up to him and say "sir can I help you. He said yes I'm looking for the owner she said this time of night he said what's it too you lady. Then she said I work here and this is kind of late for you to want to know where someone is this time of night. Then the guy ran off and she said to herself something do seem right with this guy at all. Finally she was home and she told her sister what happen and they laughed about it and carried on but Alexis still though it was weird of him to be doing that. The next morning she was getting dressed and she stopped by this bakery she loves so much to get some donuts and she saw one of her old classmates Remy and they laughed while enjoying their breakfast. I worked as a fashion designer in a famous boutique in Beverly Hills and she said to Remy girl I know that's right so how long has it been since I seen you girl she said about 7years now I believe. So are you married she said I wish I'm still waiting on Mr. Right to show up in my life girl. I know that's right.

CHAPTER 2

The next afternoon Alicia was heading to a job interview she had in Orlando and it was a manager position and she was for sure she had this job. Alexis was designing a pretty looking lace front blouse for an upcoming new artist by the name Lady Monroe. She was 25 and wow can she really sing time and time has passed Alexis noticed she forgot to take her lunch and she paused and walked to get some hot wings and fries that was her favorite. Here comes Hakeem her best friend for years lex he said she said how are you keem he said you know I'm good baby. That's good you working tonight he said you know I'm on it I have bills to pay and kids and a family to take care you know how it be. Alicia called me and told me she got the job I was proud of her she really needed and wanted that job for awhile now. I saw that same man again this time in a different store I said do you remember me from the other night he said yes. You're the nosey broad who was trying to tell me what to do I said I are you kidding me. And sir doesn't disrespect me because I can be unlady like at times. He said sit down you aren't big as a fly little one. So she smacked him to let him know she wasn't playing that crap at all. He was shocked like he couldn't believe she did that too him. She said now run them lips you bum old man you look like you belong with caged animals. Remy called her to ask her if she wanted to go the movies and she was like girl you know I'm down for a good time with you and we have to catch up on old times like we used be wilding all day in cafeteria and stuff on tables singing and dancing and rapping. Girl we used to have some good times well we all grown up now she we have to let go of the past. Alexis phone was ringing it was Hakeem and she looked down and started to smile and my keemy and answered it nicely.

CHAPTER 3

Remy said girl how you remember that girl she said we was the life of the parties and we used to have all the guys wanting us. Alexis said no honey they only liked me because I was the only girl in school who was having the dopiest stuff besides you. Remy so what happen to that guy you was so in love with lex said she said Markus man girl he was an undercover brother I found out and I was mad for years too. He could've told me the truth I wouldn't judge I had a feeling because he used to do my hair and nails a lot though. Ha-ha girl you should've know something was up with him if he was doing all that too you. Then they went to the movies to watch a new movie by Spike Lee and it was funny as heck they almost choked on their popcorn. Hakeem was blowing up my phone like crazy I said text me he said it's an emergency come now Alexis. So she ran outside the movie theatre she saw him standing there and he was like oh I'm glad you here what's up he was like I just wanted to see you. She said I though you said it was an emergency he said it was I had to see my best friend. All she could do was invite him to join them into the movies. She introduces Remy to Hakeem he was like how are you doing? She smiled and said Remy and she noticed that they were stuck on each other. Hello lex said can we watch the movie for the movie starts watching us. The movie was over and they was laughing and giggling I went to go call Alicia to see what she had going on she said nothing she said I'm about to come so hurry up and come home sis.

CHAPTER 4

We headed to the house and then Alicia opened the door for them hey everyone how was the movie she asked Alexis said girl it was good until Hakeem said it was an emergency and I ran outside like I was crazy. Then keem said girl you know you will go to the moon and back for each other she said sure will but you almost gave me a heart attack. It's time for dinner Alicia said it looks great Remy said what you cook? She said red rice, baked chicken, broccoli and cheese, and a sweet apple pie with ice cream. Hakeem said girl you be throwing down in the kitchen she said I try. Hakeem phoned rings then he said man listen I told you I'm going to have the money tomorrow so stop blowing me up. Bill collector he said you good they asked he said yes I'm alright. So Remy is it she said yes so how you know Alexis she said this was my girl back in the day then I moved and we lost contact but and I'm not going nowhere anymore I promise you that. I decided to hook up the game after dinner and we played on wiki and were dancing to a hip hop dance game. I and Hakeem was teams and licia and Remy was on teams. I said let's see how this game going to go. They started doing dancing and I was like bam, bam, yes can't touch these moves can you. Nope I and he had that dance routine down pack. Of course Alicia and Hakeem won and Alexis and Remy quit. They stayed the night and laughed and talk all night about their future plans and goals and dreams. Nothing is to hard if you believe in it Alicia said I know that's so true as long as we got god on our side we good.

CHAPTER 5

Alicia was headed to start her new job Alexis drove her they hugged kissed and said goodbye until later when she goes to pick her up. Lexis called her mom to ask her if they could to Atlanta to visit for the summer and she was bringing her friends. Her mom said that's fine sweetheart you know it's plenty of room. She said all together it is 4 so if we have to bunk we will laughing out loud. You know ya'll to grow for that. Matter of fact you have a birthday coming ma'am I said I know that big 29 whoa I'm getting up there. I will be 30 next year no man no kids and my eggs might done hatch by now. Her mother laughed child you are a mess you just have to find the right guy that's all. I said mama I guess you right well I'm going to get dressed and head to work love you she said love you too pudding pop. As she started to walk the same old man was looking into people's windows he saw her and run. Lexis said wait sir I want to apologize for hitting I was wrong but you were mean and not nice and I lost my patience can you forgive me? He said sure. Can I ask you a question without stepping on your toes he said well sure? Are you looking for some in particular or the owner. He said I wanted a job like clean up and help around the back of the store. I said I will put in a good word for you I'm a fashion designer he said I can tell you always look pretty and you have a pretty smile. Alexis blushed and said why thank you sir and you have a wonderful personality about you too. She clocked in and her boss ms Williams was there she from Africa I worked for her we was getting ready for fashion week in new York and I'm the head stylist in charge and I'm excited and ready to tear that run way up.

My designs will have them speechless some are colorful plain and unique here comes Mrs. Williams Ladies and Gentlemen we have less then 3days to present our wonderful work into fashion week. I will be looking and judging the best designs for the models to where understand back to work. Oooh lex darling could you bring me a cup of tea with lemon and your portfolio yours is the first one I'm taking a look at. She was nervous because she knew if her boss didn't like it neither wills the judges. As she was checking Alexis went back to her desk to fit a plus size model for her dress she made for her it was wonderful to see a pretty black women rock her styles and work lexis was happy and overjoyed. All of sudden Alexis you've done it again "I simply Love your work. She said thank you Mrs. Williams time to pick up my sister and she did Alicia was upset and crying lexis said wait what's wrong who do I have to beat up. She said nobody I had a rough day my heels broke and I almost fainted inside that building is hot. Girl I can't believe you passed out and you didn't call me Alexis said. Alicia said I'm okay now it just was for a few moments my coworkers came to make sure I was okay and they told me to go outside for air. Lex said well I'm glad your okay s lets go home and have some fun it is Madness Monday. Time has passed now they said you ready to party for your birthday she yes I am how about you. She said yes drinks, food, and good music, and nice looking guys yes, yes I'm over ready. Lexis said I invited Remy and Hakeem with us Alicia said what I thought it was going to be a family thing lex. I wanted to spicy the trip up some are you angry with me for that. No but we don't get to do stuff together like we used to I mean we our sisters lex. I know that she said oh licia you're jealous she said a little why because we family and blood is thicker I said I know that relax we going to have a fun trip with family and friends okay aite she said.

CHAPTER 6

Time is winding down and it's almost time to head to Atlantic City baby lex was excited Hakeem and Remy came over they was talking and asking what I have planned. I said we are going to turn up and party like there is no tomorrow and then sight see for a minute. Hakeem said Alexis I can holler at you for a second she said what's going on are you okay can I ask you for a favor? When we get back home and stuff. I said sure can you loan me $100 I swear I will pay you back I swear. I said sure I know you good for it bighead lol. He said you the best friend a guy could have for real man I thank you for everything you done for me you have heart made out of gold man. Then he kissed her on the cheeks she smiled and said awe gets your emotional but in the car. Here we go babe on our way to ATL my birthday weekend I was instagram, face book, and more pictures videos acting silly on our way there. Lexis noticed Remy was on the phone cussing and yelling and then she hanged up. Lex said you alright Remy she said they our cutting my light off tomorrow and I don't get paid until next week. She asked how much is it? Remy said $90.00 I told her I will pay it and she can pay me when she gets paid. Remy said no lexis I can't do you like that we came to have a goodtime not you take care of my issues for me. I said it's no problems you would have done the same for me right. So she it was settle she was going to help out her friends and she know they are good for the money blessed in the end because she is god will bless her always in the end.

CHAPTER 7 (BIRTHDAY WEEKEND)

They finally made it to the best place to party at atl shawty. They went to their mother house first checked in then they headed out. Alicia said aye aye lets go head to a bar for some drinks and more everyone was cool with that. Lexis order her favorite drink which is patron & pineapple juice and she had about 3 of those she was feeling good. Hakeem, Remy, Alicia was all having brown drinks lexis said yall stomach going to be hurt. All that brown will getcha down and white gets you right lol. Keem and Remy was dancing and lex was watching them and her sister said mmmmhhh now who the jealous one. She said I see the way you be looking at Hakeem lexis said what are you talking about she said do you love him more than friends she said no your crazy he my friend. I bet he is Alicia laughed and walked away but she knew her sister had like Hakeem since they was little kids. They came back to have a drink lexis said yall having fun keem said heck yea how about you lex I said you know I am. Remy pulled her to the side and said girl thanks for having my back you are the best friend ever. I said we best friends now lol I'm kidding your welcome lexis said and they hugged. Then lexis song came on and a guy asked her to dance and she looked at Hakeem he said sure he looks alright go ahead enjoy yourself birthday women. Hakeem was starring and was making sure that guy just wanted a dance. Lexis was more focus on Hakeem and they eyes was gloomy and they both smiled and looked away real fast it was a connection but they was friends. Hakeem knew down in his heart he liked Alexis but they been friends for so long he thought to himself how would I approach her with this he said I will figure out eventually he said. They all went to the dance floor and they party the night away like there was no tomorrow. Remy said it's time to head home I'm so tired and drunk Lexis said me too Hakeem said me three. Alicia was driving she was the only barely sober one and we laughed the whole way going to house. Hey mama we back she said how was the party/ how you kids say the turn up really ma let's not say that anymore. Lexis phone was going off so loud it was one of her coworkers name Kendrick he said what's up my wonderful friend she blushed and said you always call me that. She said in atl having fun with my family and friends he said I don't get know invite she said I got you when I get back home he said I will hold you to that to baby girl. Time like these she though I wish I had someone at night to make me smile like Hakeem and Kendrick but we are in friend's zone and that really sucks. The next morning we all went out for breakfast and Kendrick sent me a good morning text and it also said to my beautiful queen with that million dollar smile I can't wait until you come and be back at work. All lexis could do was think to herself like wow he really wants to see more and I know that he is a nice looking man and she is almost 30 years old next year. Everyone was eating and keem was starring straight at her and he look upset and he said who was that she said one of my coworkers checking on me. He always does he said oh he huh she said yes why oh aite lex she said is something wrong with that. He said nope your grown she said I know I am but thank you for the being concern about me too. Her mama said enough with this mushy stuff I'm full now let's go to the mall and shop and have fun while yall down here. I Florida don't have nicer mall like how we do ha-ha you got jokes huh ma.Oh ma look at this Gucci bag she said you see the price of that bag but you can afford it said I will get it or I might now I have bills to and then my Alicia said oh I love you dress you wearing I said I made it the other day. Then some young guys was walking past and was like that thing in that dress super sexy Alexis said I'm a grown women you better go play with your mama but thank you. Kendrick called while she was shopping hey sweetie she said hi how are you doing he said girl I have some good news for you someone bought your dress and she said really and he said yes and you had the price for $1,000 yeah he said this guy bought and thrown a extra 1,000 in Alexis screamed oh my god and everyone was looking like what happen lexis I said someone bough my dress I made and they left me a extra 1,000 tip yes mama. I said I can't believe it I'm so happy right now. Keem said congrats girl give me hug when he hugged her she said to herself I love the way he smells and touch me when we our close. Then Remy said I'm proud of you girl now we have to go out and celebrate this. Time was wading down it was time for us to head back to Florida and back to this money train. Lexis kissed my mama told her I love you and see you next week or month and I had a great time and they hugged her and said good bye too. Now their back on the road headed back to the sunshine state they stopped by and looked at more things. Remy said thank you for inviting us to enjoy your birthday weekend with us she said you guys are more than welcome. Alicia said lexis I need to talk to you when we get home she had a strange look in her eye she said are you okay she said sure sis. They finally made it home and everyone went home lexis said so what's going on she said I want to try to date again. Alicia for real she said yes I deserve to be happy and happy birthday again sis lexis smiled and said awe thank you sis love you.

CHAPTER 8

Lately lexis been at work and she was feeling kind of sick but she figures it was that time of month again. She remember she promise to help Remy and Hakeem out then walks Kendrick and her face started turning red he said what's up gorgeous lexis blushed and said hi how are you doing today she said not feeling good. He said ooh do you need something she said some ginger ale will be fine. He went to go get her that then walks in Hakeem hey lex lex she said hiiiiiiii she smiled he said you got the thing for me and she said dang can I call you first lol he said my bad ma. She went in her purse and she gave him the money thank you I love you for being my true friend and having my back thru it all. Of course you know how we get down he kissed her on the cheek and left. Then walks Kendrick here you go who was that guy she said my best friend for years thanks for the drink she said so softly. Kendrick was flirting with Alexis and she tried not to but she was and she was thinking to herself at least somebody spark inreast in me and she wanted it to be Hakeem but he always acted different she was thinking. Kendrick said you have a pretty smiled Alexis blushed and said thank you and you have the same as well sir. He said I can take you out sometimes she sure that would be lovely. She said yes but she was thinking she wish it was hakeem the one asking her on a date but she though kendrick seems like he a nice guy I will give him a chance. Then hakeem texted her saying I love you bighead always and forever and alexis texted love ya too handsome lol.

CHAPTER 9

She knew she couldn't stop thinking about Kendrick but in her heart she is so in love with Hakeem and he is too but he playing the tough guy act for now. Alicia was headed to her new job again and as she was catching the train this guy was giving her the good eye but she was to focus on the money. He came up to her and said may I ask you a question she said it depends on what it is. He said are you seeing someone and she said excuse me that's none of your business and she walked off. That is strange she thought to herself like the nerves of people. Lexis was in the shower and she heard the cell ring and then she step out and answered said hello who is it the voice said it's me lexis Hakeem and I was like oh hey she said and she was so excited but she tried so hard to act like she didn't care but she really do and the crazy thing was she was so in love with him. Anyways he said I need to stay with you for awhile and she said sure why what's wrong you okay? He said yes then again no I'm not I will tell you when you get here. She was worried and she was thinking to herself what could it possibly be and he arrived with his clothes in his hands and he said my mom put me out. Why she did that he said because she found out what I was doing and she said what are you doing that is so wrong. He said I can't tell you that lex foreal I can't I just know I have to watch my back on these streets from now on. She knows something wasn't stirring the pot but she said I won't dwell on it long because he wouldn't hide anything from me and we always told each other everything I mean everything she said to her. Remy was coming in the house and saw Hakeem and smiled hey keem lex said hi hun.

CHAPTER 10

Why would I be upset she said I never heard you called him that until I did and she relax girl I don't want your man. She said that's not my man he is my best friend she said yes I guess that's what your mouth say now. What is that suppose to mean lex said to Remy she said everyone and they mama knows you love Hakeem and he loves you back and yall both acting like yall don't. I said so what if I did what is to your mama she said first of all he is a handsome man if you didn't any women would love to be seen with him. Alexis said I bet you would love to be that women huh she said no I seen and know how you feel about him girl and lexis said I guess and they Remy said well okay I see you later I guess and lex said okay you do that. Alicia said what was that all about I said nothing just had to set her straight about something's she running her mouth about something she don't but everything good.

CHAPTER 11

Lately Hakeem has been coming in late and leaving early and lexis was trying to figure out why is that she said Hakeem where are you going? He said I have to handle so business I be back soon I promise she said okay. Alicia said girl he got you so wide open a blind man can find his way in there she said what are you talking about sis she said you know what I mean girl. Why not just tell the man the truth you in love with him she said I can't do that she said why not she said because we are such good friends you know.

(CHAPTER 12 THE CANCER)

Alexis was at work then she tried her best to work she did her best and then she was walking and she was like oh my god I can't deal with this she finished her work and then told her boss she has to leave early she was feeling good and needed to seek medical attention quick. Then she said I need to use the bathroom before I go though she ran quickly and she started throwing up and she saw blood and stuff and she said oh my god and as she tried to get up she was dizzy and she tried to walk to leave but she was weak. She finally got the courage and strength to get up grab the door opened and when she did she dragged herself on the floor and then Kendrick said oh shoot Alexis he yell someone called 911. Lexis what's wrong she said I was throwing up blood and she was in and out he holds on babe and she passed out. When she woke she was surrounding with her family and friends and coworkers and more. What happened she said they said you passed out and you were throwing up blood? The doctor said how you are feeling she said still in pain he said we are going to do a cat scan on her stomach and they took her back there in exam room. And 2days went by the doctor said I'm glad your family and friends are here ms Reid you have stomach cancer and it's in stage for 2 so we can due to surgery to remove and try to contain it. She paused and said I have what and started crying and she said is that means I'm going to die he said no we can catch it before it spreads but you will be on lots of meds until we do the surgery. She said thank you doctor and everyone prayed she looked at Kendrick and Hakeem they both was crying and Hakeem came kissed her on the forehead.

CHAPTER 13

Everyone was still in shock that they just found out Alexis has stomach cancer and it's not aggressive but it can spread thru her body. She was put on bed rest for 6weeks until they do what more tests and surgery she was on 6different medications and they all had different side effects and stuff. Alexis was in the bed and she was still designing and doing work from home so Hakeem came in with flowers and stuff and a card and her favorite food. She said awe keem you brought my favorite and he said you know I gotcha and then she started coughing and holding her stomach she said hand me that bottles of pills please he did. She took her meds and then he said I know you have asked me why I have been coming in lately he said I been working at this warehouse shipping and handling meds and other things for the government and stuff. What's the name of it she asked he said that's not important she said yes it is. He said I bet it is whatever man why you care so much more I'm helping with the bills aren't I she said first of all you better change the tone of your voice down okay. He said I didn't come to argue I came home on break to check on you and I will see you after work aite he kissed her on the forehead. Bye lex she said yeah bye. Her mama decided to move to help take care of her along with her sister and friend and more and she really liked that fact she was loved and had people in her corner. Cancer she said why I lord what I did wrong to deserve this she cried and couldn't understand why this was happening to her but she always stayed prayed up and know god will take care of her no matter what. Her boss came by and said we all are praying for you and she said thank you so much I really needed to hear that today.

(CHAPTER 14 THE WAITING GAME)

It's now been a month since she was diagnosed with stomach cancer and she has been trying to good. Alexis decided to go back to work she said I can't stay in this bed feeling sorry for myself and stuff. I'm going to work she said and she did the fashion show is Friday and I want to be there with my team her mother and sister didn't think that was a good idea but they felt like she is a adult and they can't hold her back from her dreams. Thursday arrived and everyone was getting prepared for tomorrow and she said Ms Williams said I want to thank everyone for the help and progress and patience and I know we got this. And to my coordinating team wonderful and lets all give Alexis a round of applause and being so strong and having a wonderful come back. Thank you everyone I'm still believing in god and I know he going to make a way for me and my family he is worthy. Kendrick called me saying can I treat you to a vacation and she said where and he says to Hawaii and she said I will get back to you on the Hun. She was so overwhelmed and couldn't believe number 1# she just found out she has cancer and she could possible die or be in pain for the rest of her life she had to react really quickly and make the most out life she thought. Life is what you make and she was determine to live it up like it's her last and does it big. Alexis knew she had to think of a backup plan if she was to not get better like who do I leave this or that too and she was so scared and all she thought was I hope I find my special someone even if it's for a while as long as I find someone to love me beyond all faults that's all she was thinking to herself. In walks Hakeem and she started smile real big like always.

CHAPTER 15

How are you feeling today? He said she said I'm feeling okay how have you been doing Mr. busy body he said I been aite you know still working hard and getting this money. She said I here that lexis he asked she said yeah what's up lex she said if something was to happen to me what would you do he said…… man lex don't even ask me that because I would lose my mind if something ever happen to my best friend, right hand, special piece of me, and more. Lexis said awe I mean that much to you she said he said more than you think then Hakeem walked into the bathroom. Remy came over and she had goodies oooh lex I have something for you she said what is it a snake lol she girl I don't play with them and she handed her the bag she said oh wow. You like it Alexis said I love its real pretty and I will wear it forever it was an 18k gold name necklace. They hugged and she said thank you so much they both hugged and Remy broke down and said I would go crazy if I lose you you're a sweet loving person lex. Lex said god knows my heart and I will be this cancer. My mom called saying are you laying down I said yes mother I am she said good I will be over later after work she said okay love you ma ma she said love you more. Then everyone decide to stay the night which was a good feeling for Alexis she loved to be surround by people who knows love her. Tomorrow is the fashion show and she prayed and said God… give me strength to do my best heal my pain and body and more and more amen. Hakeem said and he will heal one of his precious angel like you lex she smiled and said you always like being mushy don't you he said naw keeping it real with you baby girl now get some rest and we will talk more in the morning love you bf

CHAPTER 16 (THE FASHION SHOW)

Wake up everyone today is the big day the fashion show lexis was nervous she didn't sleep much she told them my stomach was bothering me but I am okay she said. She got dressed and said her prayers and she said god I trust you and love you for all things amen. Alicia, Kendrick, Remy, mama, and Hakeem was there for me. We was last to present our showcase to judges. Ms Williams said listen up we came along way and I have a surprise and she said Alexis come to the front please. Alexis walked to the front yes mama I want you to be one the models today. She looked and said me really I came prepared but I'm scared she said you got this and I said okay and I went in the back to get prepared. She went to model the dress she design and people was whispering oh my that is beautiful I love it would buy it yes she smiled to herself like bam in her mind she was like work it lex you got this girl. Then she walked off and everyone clapped they said for best designs of the year goes to Sexy Styles of Orlando Florida. We won we won everyone jumped up hugged each other lexis said we did that and they had a big trophy and at check for 15,000 and they was crown best store of the year and more and that was good Kendrick said congrats and kissed her and lexis pushed him away she said I can't I love someone else and Hakeem saw it and said really though lexis I'm out she said keem wait. Kendrick said I though you like me she said I said you're a nice guy and he apologize and left out.

CHAPTER 17

Alicia Alexis Remy went home and she was like I can't believe he walked out like that then Hakeem walked thru the door and she said keem can I talk to you he said nope I'm good. She said it's not what you think he said not what I think!!! You kissed him Alexis said no he tried to kiss me and I pushed him away you saw that. He said but you didn't want to did you lex paused and looked away he said my point proven. Lex if you want him have him aite she said Hakeem wait he said you good lex I'm gone. Remy said let me go talk to him and she said hold on slow down lexis was peeping outside and she up her window to be nosey and Remy said you know she likes him right and Hakeem said she does and Remy said yes he invited her to go on a vacation with her. Hakeem said what she said Remy said she told him I will think about it Hakeem was shocked if that's how she feel she can have him I'm done. Remy said I feel you keem he was smiling and laughing back with her and then Alexis was shocked to see that Remy wanted him and just lode on her to get Hakeem herself. She played it cool she thought to herself well that's how they want to play I will too and she said it's time to put on my game face. So then next day she called Kendrick and was like can you come by the store I want to talk to you and he said sure I can do that. So Alexis knew Hakeem was going to come by and she though well let me make him jealous. Kendrick walked in she was talking and she said I apologize for the other night. She said I was just caught off guard and he said no I apologize for coming on to you like that she said it was flattering and then walks Hakeem lexis leaned over and kissed Kendrick.

CHAPTER 18

Kendrick said wow you have soft lips Alexis said awe ken ken you do too. Hakeem walked back out and was mad Alexis said to herself I can play the game even harder ha. Remy walked over and said girl what are you doing she said minding my business and what are you doing? She said watching you kissed a guy you claim you don't like Alexis said don't worry sugar I got this. Alicia called and said girl what's wrong with Hakeem she laughed and said I don't know is something wrong. She said he came home mad as ever lexis said oh no sis I have no clue. Alexis was feeling bad inside but outside she seem like she didn't care she was shock to know Remy was backstabbing her in the back because she wanted Hakeem for herself but what Remy didn't know that Alexis heard the whole conversation last night. Lexis headed home and saw Hakeem and Remy talking outside and she stopped and looked like I know she isn't laughing all up in his face with her dragon breathe. So lexis walked passed them like it was nothing Remy said hi lex she said hi and Hakeem looked at her and said we need to talk she said naw you good enjoy your night Hakeem. Alexis took her shower and she prayed and she took her meds and she was like oh oh come on cancer stop it and then her sis walks in are you okay she you need something she said yes a hug and they hugged and she told her sis Alicia what she heard. She was like that's wrong you want me to get her Alexis said no no just continue to follow my league okay she laughed and said you know I gotcha lil sis. Then she was saying her prayers and Remy came in the room and said well I'm going home lexis said okay have a goodnight she said you too Hun and walked out. Lexis said only you know god.

CHAPTER 19

The next morning when lexis woke up she found a note saying I still want waiting for you to respond to my answers are you going on a vacation with me love Kendrick. She thought maybe I should go and get away and relax my nerves some. Alicia said hey girl how you sleep she said like a baby and she said you know she ended up staying here last night? Who Alexis said she said Remy and guess who room she in lex said Hakeem I bet she said yep. Wow she said I guess he had a fun night she said I doubt it Hakeem kept in getting up and walking around. Remy came out the room oh good morning and lexis said I though you was going home she said keem I mean Hakeem said I could've stayed lexis say he don't run nothing around here. Remy said well what's the matter lexis you think you the only one like him she said lexis said naw tramp u know you do and I know you lied on me to him but it's all good you will reap what you sow remember that. So now get your two faced self out my house before I beat the brakes off your trifling self. Remy said he fair game so just know it's on lex. She said bring it and remember this childhood friendship Hun. We will see Remy said Hakeem walked out the room and kissed Remy and said good morning angel. Alexis stood there was in a state of shocked she said well guess you enjoyed your night he said it was alright how about you she said it was wonderful and lexis stormed out. Alicia said you know you both are dead wrong and Remy you heard Alexis get out now and don't come back until we said its okay you backstabber. Hakeem said what's the issue ant she got a man Alicia said no Kendrick like her and she turned him down for you but you were so stupid to see it now you lost good women later.

CHAPTER 20 (THE TUMOR)

Meanwhile Alexis has been getting worse and worse she was at work one day and she was feeling sicker. Then she called her sister and said can you come get me I'm not feeling good she said you want to go the hospital she was like yeah I do. Then they went to the er and she was like I'm having serve pain and she told them she has cancer and they said okay and they seen her ASAP. She called her mother and coworkers to let them know where she was then Kendrick came and all she heard was that's my fiancée and she giggled to herself she said really. Then he said work with me here and she said okay I guessed. They were ready to take her back for a cat scan to see if it was spreading. All you could here was lexis screaming and then her mother was like what's going on back there she said it's okay her body is not reacting well can we admit her right away she said yes. Her mother had let her family know what was going on. Then she was in the hospital the doctors came in and said the cancer has form into a tumor and that's what's because her to have pain but he will give her meds and more until the surgery. Kendrick said when surgery is because she has a lot of pain he said in about 2months or 5weeks or at the most. He said are you kidded me sir that long. He said we will do our best and Alexis said I'm going to die aren't I and they doctors said god is man with the plan sweetheart then he kissed her forehead. She hugged Kendrick and her family she was so shocked because even though her and Hakeem beefing he could've had come she said I guess now I really see how it is and she went to sleep and rested finally.

CHAPTER 21

Day 3 in the this place she said she said I have to get out of here and back to work and Kendrick said we have to worry about your health that's more important right she looked and said right. Hakeem walked in she said mommy... he said sorry I was busy last night she said bet you was man and thanks for coming and checking on me at least you did that much. He said what's your issue I said nothing I don't want to talk anymore leave he looked and said what she yelled leave me the freak alone now!!!! He said I will let you calm down okay bye lexis. Remy came in with flowers after he left she said you got the nerve she said I didn't come to fight how are you feeling she said I'm okay having fun with Hakeem. She said I don't see what the issues we are just friends are. Alexis said yeah friends with benefits I bet. No nothing like that I just had a moment besides he loves you he called me you when we was hugging I said oh really she said but lexis he still loves my touch. Girl you better leave to and she said it won't be along till you realize it's just a friend thing between us well at least for now. She smirk bye witch and then she left smiling. The doctors came in said we got your pain under control you can go home tomorrow or today. Then Alexis she was eating breakfast and then 2hours later the doctor said Ms Reid you can go home discharges papers are ready so she was excited Kendrick was taking me home she told her mother she said okay see you there honey. Then she said thank you for being here for me ken ken he said you welcome I'm going to always be here for you if you allow me to be she just smiled and said as long as you keep it 100 with me you can be sweetheart he leaned over and kissed her she felt wonderful.

CHAPTER 22

Home sweet home she said her mother said I made you bed and favorite for you she said thank you mama. And Hakeem was in his room of course and she didn't care she replied and Kendrick said lexis if it's okay with you can I stay the night with you she said sure. Just as long you don't try no funny business he said I'm a gentlemen before anything remember that okay I have respect for you. She said here is some fresh towels and rag and soap and stuff and I'm going to take a shower then we can have dinner and some drinks so he said I will go downstairs then she said no you can relax till I get done or if you wanted too. He said it don't matter beautiful. As I was in the shower I was singing he said you have wonderful voice and I said thank you so Alexis was done and she forgot her towel she said ken darling can you hand me my towel he said I gotcha lexis. And he handed it to her and she was drying off and relaxing and then she went to go put on her night clothes and she was lotioning up and he said I can help if you like. She said thanks and he helped her and she said your hands so soft he said I used to be massage therapist wow really he said yes ma'am. Then it was a knock on the door and it was Hakeem she said I'm busy he said its important man for real. So she grabbed her robe and said I'm coming as she opened the door she saw Hakeem going downstairs she got down there and was like what then he turned around he had flowers she was shocked and said awe thank you he said I'm sorry I will not let you down ever again and he kissed her on the cheeks and he said enjoy your company babes she smiled and blushed and said okay. Then ken ken said nice flowers she said Hakeem gave them to me I love them.

CHAPTER 23

Kendrick said that was sweet he trying to butter up to you know huh she said I don't think so he is just being sweet as always he said yeah I bet he is. Then she said enough about him are you going to help with my lotion. Alexis was getting massage but she always was thinking of Hakeem she couldn't help it though she was so in love with him but didn't know how to say it. Alexis said was asleep and then she woke up to a big bang and she said ken I think someone downstairs and then he got up and said stay here. Alexis was worried he said it was just Hakeem and Remy she said oh I wonder what they doing he said cooking. She said at 3:00am she well I'm hungry too. They went down Hakeem said sorry we woke yall and he was mugging ken and she was mugging Remy. So Alexis do you guys want some steak and eggs and Hakeem I will cook lexis one I know how she likes them. Then her sister Alicia count me in to everyone was up and eating and then Alexis said I swear I can't wait for this surgery this pain is so unbearable at times and I can't take it for real. She decided to go back upstairs and have a glass of wine then there was a knock on the door she said who is it he said keemy girl. Oh come in he said you okay I will be you straight he said you know how I am I be cooling he said why you be acting like that towards me man. How you mean you the one hooking up with my friend and he said man she is cool peoples I done told you that how many times stop worrying you know I got you she said for how long. He said what's that's supposed to mean lexis I'm not getting any younger he said I know but don't rush me she said I won't but if someone else comes in and starts making me smile what you expect me do to. He said idk follow your heart lexis.

CHAPTER 24

Alexis said what's wrong with me I was having a time of my life fashion designer, friend went to Atlanta and more now I have cancer she said god why me. Then her mother walked in and say don't ever question his work he will never put more on us than we can bear. She said I know mom she was on her way to work and she stopped by her favorite café and she saw someone following her she turned around and said may I help you? He said you know a Hakeem and she said no why she said he owes up 340$ worth of drug money and if we don't get it we will start going about it differently. She said well I will pay it. He said but I though you don't know him she said I know of him he said well it don't matter. Alexis paid him he said we won't bother you again. She called him immediately I got a visit from a guy who says you owed him money Hakeem looked and said I owe people well one guy she said you owe me 450 dollars. He said you paid him she said yes he said he was going to get you I can take care of myself okay. Alexis slapped him and said you have some nerves I try helping your behind out and you do me like this I'm sick and dien I'm worried about my family, me, you and life and this what I get fine Hakeem I'm done no more okay. Hakeem said don't get upset she said no that's it if you can't do right then don't come around me period she said yes I mean it man. He was shocked and said fine I will not then he stormed out Alexis cried and then started praying she said I don't know what's gotten into him god but please keep him covered in your arms at all times and send you angels to look over him amen. She felt it but in her heart that was her king but she has to let him learn and she won't stop trying to prove her love and honesty.

CHAPTER 25

Alexis couldn't believe the man she was in love with since she been younger is treating her this way but she knows time is her side. The next day she was lying in bed she was designing from her house and clients would come there. In walks a young lady she said I'm looking for a Kendrick Alexis said he my friend may I help you. She said yes please tell him Emma Mayfield stop by Alexis said I surely will. Then hours went by Alexis was trying to figure out who this women was he came over she said ken ken can I talk to you for a minute she said sure lex how are you? She said I'm good thanking you. She said you had a visitor he said who a girl name Emma Mayfield he paused what she doing around here he asked she said I don't know. Who is she Alexis asked he said an old friend that won't leave me alone lexis said sure she is. He said you don't believe me do she said why should I huh. He said I would never lie or hurt you like how you been before. Alexis said only time will tell ken. Hakeem walks thru the front door and he said hello to Alexis she was like yeah whatever he said listen if you want me to leave forever I can she said what you see fit sir then do it. Alicia said lexis I need to talk to you for a minute lexis said if you're trying to buddy me up me aint trying to hear that. Girl come here said Alicia what lexis she said don't be this way you're sick and don't drive Hakeem away what he the one doing drugs and lien to me and whoever else sis I'm done letting him get but if he loves me he sure has a funny way of showing it and if he don't hurry up I'm going to give Kendrick a chance. He doing all things Hakeem wants to do but no he so focus on the street life and Remy face tail I'm no fool but time is on my side and god knows what I feel and I'm ready for it.

CHAPTER 26

Alexis was thinking to herself I'm in love with Hakeem and he just doesn't realize how much my heart desires him. She thought to herself I want to be able to spend my time with someone who means the world to me. Kendrick said lexis I know you been thru a lot the past months and I'm here for you in every way. You will overcome this cancer and I will be by your side. She smiled but she knows where her heart belongs at. Remy came over and she looked at Alexis and smiled and lexis said what she said nothing how are feeling she said fine okay. Remy said you don't have to be mean lex lex she said trust me you don't know the half of it. She said is Hakeem home she said nope and she said okay I will call his sell. Lexis said you have his cell too she said why not. I bet then Hakeem walked in the house and he gave Remy a fat juicy wet kiss and lexis was shocked and she looked at Hakeem and was like well since yall booed up now you and her can get out my house permantly he said I was going to move anyways. She said here some boxes dope head. He said what you call me she said you heard me your nothing but he lazy no good person and you and Remy both deserve each other. He said oh that's what you think of me now lex huh she said Hakeem you have changed and I don't even know who you are anymore just leave. GET OUT, GET OUT NOW!!!!!!!!!! She yelled he said lets go Remy and she said bye lexis and smiled Alexis tried to run after her Alicia grabbed her. I can't believe he was acting like this towards me and I don't want to see him for awhile. Alexi's mother came in and said why is Hakeem out there cussing out that poor girl lexis and Alicia looked at each other what girl? She said your friend rem remy something like that. So they ran to the window and looked and he was cussing her lol.

CHAPTER 27 (THE HAIR LOSS)

Alexis was in the shower in she washing her hair and she looked and some of her hair was in her hand and screamed no not this please god no. she said mamaaaaaaa and sis they ran what's wrong she said my hair coming out and I dried my hair it was coming out more and I said I don't like it. And then she called her doctor and told him. He said I will schedule an appointment early in the morning. She said thank you so much so for now Alexis was wearing a short hair cut and then she was so upset. The next morning some of her coworkers and her boss came by. They bought her check and she looked at her checked and was surprise she had 900 after her taxes. They said Alexis you look like you are in pain she said sometimes and then the wig was itching and she scratched it and then her wig came off and then they gasp and she said see you guys I am getting sicker they said you are still beautiful and they hugged her. Then Hakeem walks thru the door and she puts on her wig quick she said what are you doing here? He said don't worry I come to get the rest of my stuff she said here is the rest he said you even boxed it up huh. She said okay here it is you can leave now and Kendrick walks in and Alexis said hey honey he said he my queen keem said wow like that she said deuces. Hakeem looked surprised and hurt but he knew Alexis was doing this to get back at him for hurting her. So she said I want to say this I may be losing my hair but I will be this cancer only if god allows me and I will strong. So Alexis was getting ready for bed she took her wig off and said god please I want to be here help me on my journey and let me be this and god watch over Hakeem keep him shield from all harms lords knows I love him so much.

CHAPTER 28

Alexis tried to figure out why she going thru this she feels like everyone is against her. She said to herself me and Hakeem been friends since we was kids and he acting like that I losing my mind having nightmares and more. Then Alexis grabbed the phone and called Kendrick he said what's up and she said we need to talk right away and he said sure. Then he came cover Alexis was scared to tell him what's on her heart. Then as they were talking she said I think Hakeem is really done with me. He said listen man I'm so tired of Hakeem this Hakeem that you know it's getting old aite. Alexis said well excuse me that he my best friend and I care then she said aint my fault you're a lonely old person. Then Kendrick slapped Alexis she stopped and said are you crazy he said I'm so sorry she slapped him back and she said leave now now!!! She was so shock to see that Kendrick did that to her so she kept it to herself. The next morning she went out even though she aint suppose to she did. Then as she was walking into her job everyone was like lexis what are you doing here your suppose to be on bed rest and not here. It is boring in the house and I can't stay in house feeling sorry for I you know I need to get some fresh air and they smiled and said while you here let's talk about you designs. Lovely she said then she was looking at her phone she had a text from him apologizing she ignored it. I just want to be happy and beat cancer not let cancer beat me you know. She was drawing some good work until Hakeem walks in she forgot he works there now part time. He said good morning to everyone but not to Alexis and she acted liked she didn't care but deep down inside she did. As she was walking to her car she found roses on her window shield saying I'm sorry I didn't mean to hurt you forgive my queen.

CHAPTER 29

Alicia and their mother was going to be out town for a weekend and Alexis know she was going to be my herself she decided to stay over a coworker house her name was Michelle. She greeted Alexis at the door hey sexy lol she said girl stop how are you doing ms fighter she replied well I guess and you how is the baby. Michelle said she in the crib I'm going to go get her. She went to go get her and awe she was so precious Alexis though with her chubby cheeks and more and she loves kids. Michelle said what's wrong with your face you looked like you got hit she said I'm alright just side effects I guess Michelle said mmmhhh. Then they ate dinner her husband came in she said hey darling Alexis is staying the weekend with us he said great. Then watching them made Alexis think maybe one day she can have that. Then she received a text from Kendrick and she finally respond she text back…. What you want man he said I'm sorry can we have dinner she said I guess it will be okay tomorrow will be fine. The next day she met him he tried to hug her she sat down. Listen I don't want to see you no more and he looked shocked and said I said I was freaking sorry okay. I was like I made a mistake she said I hear you. They walked out he was still heated and she said you need to calm down he hit her again she said I'm calling the policed he said if you ever do I will hurt you bad. Alexis was so shocked he hit her again then she called one person that's was Hakeem. She called and he sent to voicemail and she said I guess he don't love me no more. She rushed back to her house and locked her doors. Then Kendrick said oh my I'm sorry please please don't hate me. She said leave me alone. Alexis started feeling dizzy and she fainted.

CHAPTER 30 (THE PAIN AND ABUSE)

She woke up and she said what happened he said Alexis you fainted your blood pressure dropped and Ms Reid can I ask you a question where did you get this marks from. Alexis said ohm I don't know he said is someone abusing you she looked and no no. he said let me know. He did an ultrasound he cancer was spreading and her pain was worse she said I just want to live happy doctor. So Hakeem finally called back and she said oh now you want to callback I really needed but guess you that mad huh. He said I was sleep she said I bet whatever just doesn't let you know I am in the hospital okay. He said why what happed I fainted and blood pressure dropped he said I'm on my way I said don't bother deal with your boo. Then in walks Hakeem he said what's wrong with your face she said I'm fine he said someone hitting you she said so where was you when I need a friend and an open ear. He apologize she was angry why, why, why, he hugged her I'm here now what's up she said it was Kendrick. He paused and what you are serious I be back Hakeem no what are you going to do. I got this aite I love you and you're my best friend lexis. Alexis said now you want to step up keemy I told myself I could always count on you and at some point you let me down. I'm sick and suffering and you want to now be superhero you know what no just forget it okay I can handle myself. Hakeem paused and said you act like someone hurted you lex. If I couldn't recall didn't ole boy liked and you liked him so what didn't you smash remy he paused. I'm going thru it you know Alexis took of her wig look Hakeem look I'm losing my hair Kendrick hits me I have cancer you be trading me. I can't handle this anymore I'm done with everything I need a vacation I'm over this man.

CHAPTER 31

Alexis called everyone and she said listen everyone knows what I'm going thru and she said I want to say it's getting harder and harder and I need time away from everyone for awhile. I'm going on a vacation for a 2weeks or a month to clear my head. Alicia and her mother said why so long she said I have to deal with something's on my own okay and I need peace and quiet from everyone and everything. Alexis went in her room and she was booking a vacation to Rome for 2weeks and she did she said to herself lord I and really need this and you right now to help me. Then there was a knock on the door it was Hakeem she said what you want man he said why you sound like you have so much angry and hurt in your heart. She said I just need to get away from people. He kissed her and said listen lex I'm sorry I haven't been there for you I love you with all my soul and heart and I'm sorry if I let you down in ways. She looked and said I forgive you Hakeem but I still need to get away and clear my head. I leave in the morning could you drive me he said sure. So Alexi's mom called her downstairs and she said we understand you're going thru a lot right now and we want you to know we are here for you in every way. So she handed Alexis an envelope she said oh my you guys didn't have to do this we wanted too. So lex hugged everyone and they ate dinner then they left and she went upstairs to take a bubble bath and she realized how much it was it was 400$ she said to herself this spending money. Then there was a knock on the door she said who is it he said Hakeem she said come in. he was like can we talk she said I guess he said I want you to know the only reason I kissed remy because I was jealous of you Kendrick. She said do you love me he said yes with all my heart and soul lex.

CHAPTER 32 (THE VACATION/ EMERAGENCY

Then she said why you treated me like that then he said you were all up on him how you think that made me feel. Alexis said keemy really you started talking to her way before I paid Kendrick any attention. He said I will still see his behind for putting hands on you whoa whoa wait and lex you mean to tell me you didn't hit back you know I did but he is stronger than me. So she got out the tub and went in her room Hakeem was downstairs Alexis said her prayers and she does her usually ask god to pray for her and everyone. The next morning she got up she showered and was ready to go she seen where Hakeem had fallen asleep in his room. She said keemy wake up my plan leave in 2hours. He got up and she made breakfast and then hour later she hugged her mother and sister and said I see you guys in a week or 2 and I love you guys dearly. They hugged each other tightly. Lexis left and Hakeem helped her with her bags and he looked and said Alexis I want you to remember no matter what I love you with all my heart and always will she said I know love you to bighead they hugged and she bordered her plane. She was first class she said lord knows I could you this vacation. She arrived in Rome she said yes this is so beautiful she was a nice hotel 5star and she called everyone to let them know she made it there safely. Then she got an email Hakeem I miss you already and I want you to know I have a surprise for you when you get back and she reply okay keemy lol. Alexis was in her hotel and she was enjoying her vacation she had room service nice site seeing and more. She was in her room and she was thinking to herself I can't believe I'm in one of the most beautiful cities in the world. Then she got a text from Kendrick saying listen I know I messed up but you have to forgive me. She said leave me alone.

CHAPTER 33

She said listen I made my decision I know who I want to be with and you're not the one for me okay. He said you know I love you and I'm so sorry. Alexis said you don't love me you just didn't want me with Hakeem. I know where my heart belongs and it belongs with Hakeem and that's final. Kendrick said I can't believe you would pick him over me she said yes now goodbye. Alexis was happy she decided to follow her heart she was in the shower and she felt dizzy and she step out the shower and she was saying oh my god not today I far away from home god not today. She tried video chat her sister she is connected all she could say was help. They were scared Alexis was able to get to the phone she knew it little bit of the language and they understood her. Alexis was now in a hospital in Rome and her family was on the first flight there and she was sick and stuff and she was released. Alexis said to herself really devil I can't even have a good time without you trying to take my joy. So she packed up and headed home after only being there 3days they got back home 12hours later. She went straight to her doctor he said Ms Reid I want to put you on blood thinners okay and more chemo okay. Then she said I am really tired of all this honestly but I will okay he said I know but you will pull thru. Alexis felt as though she was getting worst she said I want to become a organ donor in case something happens to me I could save some else life in return. Alexis was home now she was talking to Hakeem and he was cuddled up with her and she said keemy. He said yea baby girl what's up she said whatever happens to me I want you to know I love you and you are my sunshine you make me happy when skies are grey. He said I love you to my queen get some rest and you know I never love nobody but you lexis I promise you that.

CHAPTER 34   (DECISION/ LOVE MAKING)

Alexis woke up the next morning and she looked over and realized it was Hakeem and she kissed him on the lips she said good morning he said smiled and said how are you feeling? She said I'm feeling okay thank you for being here for me. Hakeem said no you know I'm here and I will never let you go lex lex. Alexis felt so happy to know Hakeem was in her corner. They went downstairs and she said I can try to make breakfast he said no I got it babes she said are you sure yes. Then there was a knock on the door that is it then the voice said remy and lexis answered May I help you? Remy said no you may not I'm here looking for Hakeem and she saw him starring in the kitchen she walked up and tried to kiss him he said naw naw. He said listen remy sorry if I led you on but I'm not going to play these games with you I know where my heart belongs and it's with Alexis for real. Alexis said oh little old me. And Alexis stood up and see remy with your stupid self we have history and I'm loyal real and really loves him you don't. Remy said oh I see how it is she said Alexis trust me I wasn't trying to be shady but Hakeem sure knows how to make a girl feel special. Girl bye you was a one night stand remy said you think so we will see. There is the door now use it tramp she said two can play this game. Bye baby she said to Hakeem he didn't answer lexis smiled ha. Then Alexis went upstairs and she started thinking maybe he is putting on a front for me how do I know. Time will tell I hope he isn't said lexis to her. He walks in and said trust me I'm not Alexis you been my special friend for years. Alexis said is that all I am to you is a friend he said no you're my boo I just want you to know and realize that okay and I will never ever leave your side you know that lexis.

CHAPTER 34

Her sister was coming home from work and stopped in she called Alexis and said I'm at your favorite café do you want something she said yes get me some coffee and doughnuts she said I got you. Then Alicia looked over and she saw remy talking to kenerdrick then she texted Alexis telling her and Alicia said I'm going to follow them. So she did and she said girl the both are headed to a hotel. Then Alicia came home and she was like I wonder what they got going on the probably planning something. Hey ma that's what they told they mother as she came home she said her babies how are yall doing? They both said well. She said I have some good news and bad news I might have to move back to Atlanta and they both said why. She said I got offer a bigger and better position. Alexis said I don't want to move my life is here in Florida. She said I will have to think about and plus I have Hakeem here what am I going to do if we move then what then her mom said talk to him about it and see what he says about it. She called Hakeem the next day and she said we have to talk and she told him about what her mom said and he was like dang then what you decide to do. He said I will discuss it with you later. Then he said I will run you a bubble bath she said that would nice. So she entered the room he had rose petals on the bed and slow music playing he was in the tub with her too they cuddle up and started kissing and hugging. He picked her up and carried her to the bed and they made love and he whispered I love you and she said I love you too and they both looked into each other eyes and said I have a question for you she said yes he said will you have my baby be the mother of our child. She said yes I will and then the sun came up they was smiling.

CHAPTER 35

They was both was standing up and looking at the sun with the sheets wrapped around them she said oh that was amazing keemy. He said you was to lexis dang girl all that. She said yeah I got it like that then she smiled. She said did you mean what you said about me being the mother of your children one day he said yes I do and I made my decision. Alexis said oh what's that then he said I will love to move with you to Atlanta if you moved. She looked and paused and said really you would baby. He said of course I love you and you are my everything and where you wannabe is where I want to be always and forever aite. Thank you so much and she kissed him and he said I'm going to take a shower so I can get ready for work. Alexis was thinking to herself I feel somewhat complete I have the best friend/ man in the world that means so much to me and he I know he loves me back. Michelle texted me saying hey Alexis when you get a chance I need you to call me back ASAP. Her lexis ran to downstairs to her house phone and called Michelle she said everything okay. She said no do you know who a Kendrick is Alexis said yeah why well he left a package her for you. Alexis said I will be right over to get it and I told Hakeem and he said naw lets go together. They arrive there and Michelle was outside it was a brown paper box I said knowing him it's probably a bomb then we took and counted to 3and we opened it I was very differently kind of color roses and then we look down and it was money and it had the total. 45, 00 we both looked and we said wow. Then we still paused and tried to figure out why did he give this too Alexis said I don't trust keemy put it down I'm going to give him ring.

CHAPTER 36

Kendrick this is Alexis how are you he said I'm doing good now I get to hear your voice my angel. Alexis said I got your package and what is and who is all the money for she said. He said for you my queen I'm trying to show you I can give you the finer things in life not that young knuckle head. She said thank you for the floors they are beautiful but as for the money I'm returning it he said no I want you to keep it. And he didn't even realize she was recording it and she says is this a gift he said yes a gift and you don't have to pay me back at all. Alexis said well okay if you say so then he said one more favor please can we have dinner. Alexis said ken listen he said please one last time. She said hold on let me look at my dates then she looked at Hakeem he shooked his head and was like say yea. Alexis said how does Friday at 7ish sounds he said perfect and lexis baby but your Sunday best okay she looked at the phone and said okay I will bye. Alicia said girl what you going to do you got two men in love with you she said but I know where your heart belongs at it's with Hakeem isn't it Alexis looked and smiled and said you know it is but I he still says you're my special best friend. Friend and I'm like we been friends for years if you love me like you say you do why not say girlfriend or ask me. It takes time Alicia said well I hope it be very soon because I'm tired of being in a friend zone if he wants to be a part of my life more and more he better step up. Then here comes Friday she was getting all dressed up Alicia said where you going all dressed up she said I have a date. Then when she walks outside there was a limo she said wow all this really she said I hope this aint no type of crazy thing ken got.

CHAPTER 37

Alexis said I know he didn't go thru all this for one last date as she entered the limo there was kenerdick in the limo too she said all this for one night really. He said yes anything for you my queen she said stop it okay of course then they arrived at a nice fancy restaurant and she said we going here. He said well of course only the best for you Alexis and she smiled and said that's really nice and then when she walked in her saw roses leading to their table. He said order how many or whatever you want are you sure? yes he said Alexis I know I made mistakes and I want you to know I worked on my angry and I took classes and I learn my lesson. She said I bet you have and he said I swear and she said okay we will see. She said to the waitress I will have a steak well done with grilled shrimp basted with garlic and parmesan cheese a chef salad and a bottle of pink mascato please. And for you sir he said the same accept my steak med-rare. That will be all and he pulled out a box and she said by the way what am I suppose to do about the money he said whatever you like. Then he pulled out another pink box he knew she loved pink she said what is it. He said opened it and when she did it was a pretty pink diamond she said oh my goodness ken ken I mean Kendrick he said what baby. She said it's so beautiful he said it's yours and she said I can't accept it and he said sure you can think of it a friendship and apology ring okay she said okay I will. And they started to eat and she couldn't stop looking at it she said how am I going to explain this he said you are a grown adult you don't have to explain nothing to nobody baby girl it's between me and you okay. He said do you want to stay over tonight she said sure I would like that and she smiled :0).

CHAPTER 38 (CRAZY DATE)

They arrived to his house she my you have a wonderful home and he said thank you it sometimes gets lonely up here with no women you know. She said sorry to hear that. He said that's why I want you Alexis Reid. Alexis said I told you my heart belongs to Hakeem. Kendrick said you are holding on to someone who always going to see you as a friend everyone sees it Alexis why you can't. Alexis said that's not true he always tells me he loves me and I'm his special friend…… he said my point proven you deserve more than that I can give that too you. She said I can't cant I'm sorry then she grabbed her coat and she was leaving he said listen to me and he grabbed her by the wrist tightly remember this I am the man for you and one day you will be mind Alexis said I know you aint change. She threw the ring back him. And she went home and Hakeem was up waiting he said what's wrong she said Hakeem it started off good and then he got crazy telling me I will be his one day. Hakeem said I need to handle him once and for all. She said what are you going to do Hakeem said have a man to man talk with him. Alexis said please be careful babe he said I will and he kissed her on the face. Alexis had appointment the next morning and she was going to go with Hakeem but he said I have to go see my kids and go check Kendrick. So Hakeem went to go check on his little ones they was doing good he called then told me I'm going to go see him at his job. He pulled up and saw him talking to a client aye bra and Kendrick turned around a chuckle what you want Youngblood. He said I'm going to say this and I'm going to make this clear leave Alexis alone she don't want you and she is in love with me. Then Kendrick said listen I really love her you don't even deserve her.

CHAPTER 39

Hakeem said you think I don't we moving to Atlanta together she told you that man he said funny when we was together she never mention you. Kendrick said did she tell you about the pink diamond ring I gave her and she loved it. Hakeem paused naw she didn't he said my point I can love her and he said you hit her to don't ever come around her again bra I mean it. Kendrick said I aint going nowhere then he pulled out a gun listen…….. I will have Alexis Reid she is my everything and I will make her mind and not even you will stop me. So gone get out here for I leave you leaking now. This aint over I promise you that Kendrick said I will be waiting. So he went back to the house to find Alexis on her laptop and he walks in the room and says let me talk to you she said sure wait wait a minute what's wrong with you. So be 100 did he offer you a pink diamond ring she said yes but I told him no I don't want it I want you and he said that's not what he said. Alexis said I don't care what he says that's the true I told him I love you and he got mad I told you that. Then Hakeem says do you love me lex or am I just someone to keep around. She slaps him how dare you speak to me that way he said I need to know am I the guy for you or no. she said I should be asking you that. Me oh lexis you're my special friend. Listen I didn't mean to upset you I'm asking she said to late then if you don't believe me or think I love you why are always here and telling me you love me Hakeem because if you don't then go back to remy or baby mama because I'm not going to play this cat and mouse games with you I'm not I'm not!!! He said lexis I'm sorry it's not like that I promise you okay I'm here for you only and you love you Alexis Reid she said yeah Hakeem we will see I love you more.

CHAPTER 40 (The Coma)

Alexis had so many thoughts going thru her head she working herself a lot and lately she been down and dizzy and Alexis was in the kitchen and she found herself on the floor and she ended up hitting her head and then Hakeem happen to come home and he was talking to her but she couldn't respond. Alexis was saying to herself I can see him but I can't hear him then she passed out. Her mother arrived and Alexis was in a coma from what the doctor said and her mother was like for how long he said could be weeks, months, even, years. Alicia said ma I can't stand to see her like this ma. Hakeem was there and he was saying man lexis please don't leave please I love you and I will always be here for you I swear. If you can hear me move open your eyes he said I will do whatever you want I'll marry you we can be a family please. Then the doctor walks in and he said son let her rest if she hears god will give you sign. And everyone went back home Alicia, their mother, Kendrick, and even remy was their they was praying and Alicia said what are we going to do if she don't make it Hakeem said please don't say that she said I'm sorry okay then Kendrick said yeah I hope my baby girl okay Hakeem said aye on everything she is not you baby girl your boo nothing she is my girl my world and I told you stay away from her and they started arguing and Alexis mother said stop it stop it now and they apologize this is not what she be wanting this. Then Hakeem went back to the hospital and he was praying he said I know you're going to pull thru I just know it lex lex you liked when I called you when you wake up I will say that for you and he kissed her on the forehead he the doctor came in and said son I can see she means a lot to hakeem said she does she does.

CHAPTER 41

The doctor said son listen sometimes we let people get away and we don't say how we feel you never no she might be able to be hearing you it's up to the person body. He said I watch you come in here 3days straight looking like you hasn't sleep yet. I prove for you to stay the night whenever you want and so are her other family. Hakeem shooked his hands and said thank you doctor. So he called and told them what the doctors said so Alexis and Alicia mother stayed the first night and remy and Kendrick stayed one night and Hakeem stayed the rest. One morning Hakeem saw Kendrick going into the hospital with yellow roses. Alexis loves daises and pink red and any color rose. So he forgot him and Alexis had that stash of money in a safe in her room. So he went and took out 300$ he went to the gift shop and got her card teddy bear, and pink yellow white and red roses and the nurse Keisha said my Hakeem you are such a thoughtful young man he said she is my soon to be wife. Kendrick said well we will see Hakeem said not today if you're not here for here then leave. Kendrick said it's only a matter of time before she wakes up to the better man. Hakeem shrugs and said your right partner and I will be here waiting for her. Then the doctors came in to change her tubes. Then he started saying I drew this for you Alexis and I hope you like it baby.

HAKEEM & ALEXIS 4LIFE XOXO

HAKEEM & ALEXIS 4LIFE XOXO

CHAPTER 42

Hakeem went home after a staying there back and forth and he was exhausted Alicia said you need to eat something you look weak. He said I feel a little that way but I can't leave her side licia. She said I understand but here is what I learned love endures all things, love is patient, love is kind trust me Alexis knows how much you love her and god does too. Here is my thing we all grew up together and yall had something since then why you nevered made move he said I'm going to be real I was scared I didn't think she liked me he said Alicia said really lol well I knew a little bit but I wasn't for sure. Well she does and when she makes it out alive I hope you do the right thing because I been watching Kendrick he is going to ask her to marry him and then what he said trust I have a plan. It's been now a month and Alexis is still in a coma and the doctor said well we all have to continue to pray now and her family gathered around started singing her favorite church songs. One was Pass Me Not and Take Me Back and Lord I need Thee. Hakeem had started crying and holding her hand said lex lex I want you to know god will see us thru this I have faith. I even got re baptize and everything is going too alright. The doctor said that's nice son and he said visiting hours are almost over whoever staying let me know Alicia said I am tonight and Hakeem said I will tomorrow he said it's okay you can too.hakeem went downstairs to get dinner. Alicia said Alexis pooh remember me always saying that and you be like bissh please she said come on little sis please please wake up mommy stressing Hakeem crying and praying and changing his life and I'm staying strong for us. I know you're okay because daddy always said my girls are fighters always you know. I want you to hear me lil sis I love you and I need you sis please.

CHAPTER 43

Now it's like it's a waiting game. Alicia started crying and begging please sis wake up wake up your just dreaming ohhhhhhhh… please wake up for me mommy Hakeem and everyone that loves you. She said this is just a test and we will learn to appearciate you more and Hakeem said come on licia she wouldn't want us to be crying so much. The next morning Alicia went to work and so did Hakeem. The doctors lets go take her blood pressure. Doctor Ray said I know you may not be able to hear me but u I hope you can. Sweetheart you have a wonderful family that loves and a young man that is deeply in love with you. I heard so much good things about you and how you're a wonderful designer friend daughter and more I'm also praying for you and god just having a wonderful talk with him honey wake up soon and make you family whole again. Hakeem walks in the beautiful aint she he said yes and excuses me I have another patient to deal with. He walked over to her good afternoon baby I bought you more roses. I got your room looking like a flower shop. He I got your favorite for dinner tonight bacon cheeseburger w cheese fries and pecan ice cream. I know you would be been like give me some keemy and I would be like girl nooo!!!! Then ask he was saying it the doctor said can we I talk to you and he said we will keep her for 1more month then if not we will call hospice if the swelling goes down she can wake up and try to recover day by day okay he said no no man. Hakeem called and told the family what the doctors says. I know she going to wake up Hakeem started rubbing her feet with lotion and he said I know you like that. Next month has come and Alexis still was in a coma but her swelling was going down a little bit and that was good.

CHAPTER 44 (Alexis opens her eyes)

The next morning Hakeem was sleeping and he looked and Alexis was attempting to open her eyes and she did and Hakeem smiled he said lex lex oh god thank you hi baby how are you. She blinked and opened her mouth and said I feel sore but what happened. Hakeem called doctor ray. He came in he said well good morning and welcome back she said where did I go. He said about a month an ago you had a nasty fall and you were in a coma for about 2months now. She said I was then Alicia and their mom got down there and said hi baby I'm so glad you are okay and I know god was watching over you. Alexis had sat up in the bed and she said ooohhhh my back sore and my head. He said you have been stiff for quite awhile Hakeem said I can massage you. she was washing off in her bed Hakeem was helping her and the door was locked and he said I'm so glad you are okay lex baby I swear if I would've lose you I wouldn't know what to do for real you are my heart. She said oh I am he said yes and I have a surprise for you later on today. Alexis was up and eating and the nurses her mother sister remy and Hakeem came in the weight team had put her in the wheelchair. Hakeem said Alexis princess Reid we been best friends since childhood you are my life line my queen my world my heart beat knowing I almost lost you that's something I can't never forgot. I want to walk and continue to walk this journey with you forever. Will you marry me and be my queen for the rest of our life. Alexis paused and she said wowwwww and she looked and said yes I will marry you and everyone clapped and she was crying then she whispered to him about time he said I know bighead I love you lex.

CHAPTER 50 (THE SURPRISE OF HER LIFE)

Alexis was finally going home she and Hakeem was doing great they had a wedding to plan and she decided she is going to be happy and follow her heart. Her and Hakeem wedding was set a year from now. They were happier than ever. Remy and Kendrick surprise got together. Alicia said I get to be a maid of honor and mom matron I said of course. Hakeem was doing well on his job Alexis had appointment at the doctors the next weekend. The doctors said how you been she said I been feeling quezzy a little bit he said well that is normal for cancer patient. She said how is my tumor he said honestly they have shrunken that's good. He said if you keep this up you might beat this Alexis smiled. Kenerdrick came by he said Alexis I want to say sorry for everything and I wish you the best on your engagement Alexis hugged him and said all is forgiving and then Hakeem walked in. kenerdrick held out his hand and Hakeem shook it he said you're the right the better man did win. So Alexis went in the room and Hakeem followed her she went to lay down he said you ready to be Mrs. Walters she said yes I am. Alexi's doctors called her saying come early in the morning he have some news and she said okay doctors. I will she said I wonder what it is he said I hope its good news. So they cuddled the whole night she said thank you for never giving up on me and loving me he said I knew I was going to marry ever since I first layed eyes on you. You put up with me Alexis thru all my BS and street life and I love you now and forever love you to keemy our love is unbreakable and strong and forever. The next morning the doctor said I'm happy for and your expecting a baby as well to be continue............

Made in the USA
Coppell, TX
14 March 2022

74937244R00031